Conference on Empirical Methods in Natural Language Processing 2019 and the 9th International Joint Conference on Natural Language Processing (EMNLP-IJCNLP)

Tutorial Abstracts

Hong Kong, China
3-7 November 2019

ISBN: 978-1-7138-0069-9

Printed from e-media with permission by:

Curran Associates, Inc.
57 Morehouse Lane
Red Hook, NY 12571

Some format issues inherent in the e-media version may also appear in this print version.

Printed with permission by Curran Associates, Inc. (2020)

Association for Computational Linguistics
209 N. Eighth Street
Stroudsburg, Pennsylvania 18360

Phone: 1-570-476-8006
Fax: 1-570-476-0860

acl@aclweb.org

Additional copies of this publication are available from:

Curran Associates, Inc.
57 Morehouse Lane
Red Hook, NY 12571 USA
Phone: 845-758-0400
Fax: 845-758-2633
Email: curran@proceedings.com
Web: www.proceedings.com

TABLE OF CONTENTS

Bias and Fairness in Natural Language Processing

Kai-Wei Chang, Vinod Prabhakaran, Vicente Ordonez

Abstract

Recent advances in data-driven machine learning techniques (e.g., deep neural networks) have revolutionized many natural language processing applications. These approaches automatically learn how to make decisions based on the statistics and diagnostic information from large amounts of training data. Despite the remarkable accuracy of machine learning in various applications, learning algorithms run the risk of relying on societal biases encoded in the training data to make predictions. This often occurs even when gender and ethnicity information is not explicitly provided to the system because learning algorithms are able to discover implicit associations between individuals and their demographic information based on other variables such as names, titles, home addresses, etc. Therefore, machine learning algorithms risk potentially encouraging unfair and discriminatory decision making and raise serious privacy concerns. Without properly quantifying and reducing the reliance on such correlations, broad adoption of these models might have the undesirable effect of magnifying harmful stereotypes or implicit biases that rely on sensitive demographic attributes.In this tutorial, we will review the history of bias and fairness studies in machine learning and language processing and present recent community effort in quantifying and mitigating bias in natural language processing models for a wide spectrum of tasks, including word embeddings, co-reference resolution, machine translation, and vision-and-language tasks. In particular, we will focus on the following topics:+ Definitions of fairness and bias.+ Data, algorithms, and models that propagate and even amplify social bias to NLP applications and metrics to quantify these biases.+ Algorithmic solutions; learning objective; design principles to prevent social bias in NLP systems and their potential drawbacks.The tutorial will bring researchers and practitioners to be aware of this issue, and encourage the research community to propose innovative solutions to promote fairness in NLP.

Anthology ID:

D19-2004

Data Collection and End-to-End Learning for Conversational AI

Tsung-Hsien Wen, Pei-Hao Su, Paweł Budzianowski, Iñigo Casanueva, Ivan Vulić

Abstract

A fundamental long-term goal of conversational AI is to merge two main dialogue system paradigms into a standalone multi-purpose system. Such a system should be capable of conversing about arbitrary topics (Paradigm 1: open-domain dialogue systems), and simultaneously assist humans with completing a wide range of tasks with well-defined semantics such as restaurant search and booking, customer service applications, or ticket bookings (Paradigm 2: task-based dialogue systems).The recent developmental leaps in conversational AI technology are undoubtedly linked to more and more sophisticated deep learning algorithms that capture patterns in increasing amounts of data generated by various data collection mechanisms. The goal of this tutorial is therefore twofold. First, it aims at familiarising the research community with the recent advances in algorithmic design of statistical dialogue systems for both open-domain and task-based dialogue paradigms. The focus of the tutorial is on recently introduced end-to-end learning for dialogue systems and their relation to more common modular systems. In theory, learning end-to-end from data offers seamless and unprecedented portability of dialogue systems to a wide spectrum of tasks and languages. From a practical point of view, there are still plenty of research challenges and opportunities remaining: in this tutorial we analyse this gap between theory and practice, and introduce the research community with the main advantages as well as with key practical limitations of current end-to-end dialogue learning.The critical requirement of each statistical dialogue system is the data at hand. The system cannot provide assistance for the task without having appropriate task-related data to learn from. Therefore, the second major goal of this tutorial is to provide a comprehensive overview of the current approaches to data collection for dialogue, and analyse the current gaps and challenges with diverse data collection protocols, as well as their relation to and current limitations of data-driven end-to-end dialogue modeling. We will again analyse this relation and limitations both from research and industry perspective, and provide key insights on the application of state-of-the-art methodology into industry-scale conversational AI systems.

Anthology ID:

D19-2003

Discreteness in Neural Natural Language Processing

Lili Mou, Hao Zhou, Lei Li

Abstract

This tutorial provides a comprehensive guide to the process of discreteness in neural NLP.As a gentle start, we will briefly introduce the background of deep learning based NLP, where we point out the ubiquitous discreteness of natural language and its challenges in neural information processing. Particularly, we will focus on how such discreteness plays a role in the input space, the latent space, and the output space of a neural network. In each part, we will provide examples, discuss machine learning techniques, as well as demonstrate NLP applications."Graph-based Deep Learning in Natural Language Processing Shikhar Vashishth, Naganand Yadati and Partha Talukdar This tutorial aims to introduce recent advances in graph-based deep learning techniques such as Graph Convolutional Networks (GCNs) for Natural Language Processing (NLP). It provides a brief introduction to deep learning methods on non-Euclidean domains such as graphs and justifies their relevance in NLP. It then covers recent advances in applying graph-based deep learning methods for various NLP tasks, such as semantic role labeling, machine translation, relationship extraction, and many more.Semantic Specialization of Distributional Word Vectors Goran Glavaś, Edoardo Maria Ponti and Ivan Vulić "Distributional word vectors have become an indispensable component of most state-of-art NLP models. As a major artefact of the underlying distributional hypothesis, distributional word vector spaces conflate various paradigmatic and syntagmatic lexico-semantic relations. For example, relations such as synonymy/similarity (e.g., car-automobile) or lexical entailment (e.g., car-vehicle) often cannot be distinguished from antonymy (e.g., black-white), meronymy (e.g., car-wheel) or broader thematic relatedness (e.g., car-driver) based on the distances in the distributional vector space. This inherent property of distributional spaces often harms performance in downstream applications, since different lexico-semantic relations support different classes of NLP applications. For instance, Semantic Similarity provides guidance for Paraphrasing, Dialogue State Tracking, and Text Simplification, Lexical Entailment supports Natural Language Inference and Taxonomy Induction, whereas broader thematic relatedness yields gains for Named Entity Recognition, Parsing, and Text Classification and Retrieval.A plethora of methods have been proposed to emphasize specific lexico-semantic relations in a reshaped (i.e., specialized) vector space. A common solution is to move beyond purely unsupervised word representation learning and include external lexico-semantic knowledge, in a process commonly referred to as semantic specialization. In this tutorial, we provide a thorough overview of specialization methods, covering: 1) joint specialization methods, which augment distributional learning objectives with external linguistic constraints, 2) post-processing retrofitting models, which fine-tune pre-trained distributional vectors to better reflect external linguistic constraints, and 3) the most recently proposed post-specialization methods that generalize the perturbations of the post-processing methods to the whole distributional space. In addition to providing a comprehensive overview of specialization methods, we will introduce the most recent developments, such as (among others): handling asymmetric relations (e.g., hypernymy-hyponymy) in Euclidean and hyperbolic spaces by accounting for vector magnitude as well as for vector distance; cross-lingual transfer of semantic specialization for languages without external lexico-semantic resources; downstream effects of specializing distributional vector spaces; injecting external knowledge into unsupervised pretraining architectures such as ELMo or BERT.

Anthology ID:

D19-2005

Dive into Deep Learning for Natural Language Processing

Haibin Lin, Xingjian Shi, Leonard Lausen, Aston Zhang, He He, Sheng Zha, Alexander Smola

Abstract

Deep learning has become the dominant approach to NLP problems, especially when applied on large scale corpora. Recent progress on unsupervised pre-training techniques such as BERT, ELMo, GPT-2, and language modeling in general, when applied on large corpora, is shown to be effective in improving a wide variety of downstream tasks. These techniques push the limits of available hardware, requiring specialized frameworks optimized for GPU, ASIC, and distributed cloud-based training.A few complexities pose challenges to scale these models and algorithms effectively. Compared to other areas where deep learning is applied, these NLP models contain a variety of moving parts: text normalization and tokenization, word representation at subword-level and word-level, variable-length models such as RNN and attention, and sequential decoder based on beam search, among others.In this hands-on tutorial, we take a closer look at the challenges from these complexities and see how with proper tooling with Apache MXNet and GluonNLP, we can overcome these challenges and achieve state-of-the-art results for real-world problems. GluonNLP is a powerful new toolkit that combines MXNet's speed, the flexibility of Gluon, and an extensive new library automating the most laborious aspects of deep learning for NLP.

Anthology ID:

D19-2001

Graph-based Deep Learning in Natural Language Processing

Shikhar Vashishth, Naganand Yadati, Partha Talukdar

Abstract

This tutorial aims to introduce recent advances in graph-based deep learning techniques such as Graph Convolutional Networks (GCNs) for Natural Language Processing (NLP). It provides a brief introduction to deep learning methods on non-Euclidean domains such as graphs and justifies their relevance in NLP. It then covers recent advances in applying graph-based deep learning methods for various NLP tasks, such as semantic role labeling, machine translation, relationship extraction, and many more.

Anthology ID:

D19-2006

Processing and Understanding Mixed Language Data

Monojit Choudhury, Anirudh Srinivasan, Sandipan Dandapat

Abstract

Multilingual communities exhibit code-mixing, that is, mixing of two or more socially stable languages in a single conversation, sometimes even in a single utterance. This phenomenon has been widely studied by linguists and interaction scientists in the spoken language of such communities. However, with the prevalence of social media and other informal interactive platforms, code-switching is now also ubiquitously observed in user-generated text. As multilingual communities are more the norm from a global perspective, it becomes essential that code-switched text and speech are adequately handled by language technologies and NUIs.Code-mixing is extremely prevalent in all multilingual societies. Current studies have shown that as much as 20% of user generated content from some geographies, like South Asia, parts of Europe, and Singapore, are code-mixed. Thus, it is very important to handle code-mixed content as a part of NLP systems and applications for these geographies.In the past 5 years, there has been an active interest in computational models for code-mixing with a substantive research outcome in terms of publications, datasets and systems. However, it is not easy to find a single point of access for a complete and coherent overview of the research. This tutorial is expecting to fill this gap and provide new researchers in the area with a foundation in both linguistic and computational aspects of code-mixing. We hope that this then becomes a starting point for those who wish to pursue research, design, development and deployment of code-mixed systems in multilingual societies.

Anthology ID:

D19-2002

Semantic Specialization of Distributional Word Vectors

Goran Glavaś, Edoardo Maria Ponti, Ivan Vulić

Abstract

Distributional word vectors have become an indispensable component of most state-of-art NLP models. As a major artefact of the underlying distributional hypothesis, distributional word vector spaces conflate various paradigmatic and syntagmatic lexico-semantic relations. For example, relations such as synonymy/similarity (e.g., car-automobile) or lexical entailment (e.g., car-vehicle) often cannot be distinguished from antonymy (e.g., black-white), meronymy (e.g., car-wheel) or broader thematic relatedness (e.g., car-driver) based on the distances in the distributional vector space. This inherent property of distributional spaces often harms performance in downstream applications, since different lexico-semantic relations support different classes of NLP applications. For instance, Semantic Similarity provides guidance for Paraphrasing, Dialogue State Tracking, and Text Simplification, Lexical Entailment supports Natural Language Inference and Taxonomy Induction, whereas broader thematic relatedness yields gains for Named Entity Recognition, Parsing, and Text Classification and Retrieval.A plethora of methods have been proposed to emphasize specific lexico-semantic relations in a reshaped (i.e., specialized) vector space. A common solution is to move beyond purely unsupervised word representation learning and include external lexico-semantic knowledge, in a process commonly referred to as semantic specialization. In this tutorial, we provide a thorough overview of specialization methods, covering: 1) joint specialization methods, which augment distributional learning objectives with external linguistic constraints, 2) post-processing retrofitting models, which fine-tune pre-trained distributional vectors to better reflect external linguistic constraints, and 3) the most recently proposed post-specialization methods that generalize the perturbations of the post-processing methods to the whole distributional space. In addition to providing a comprehensive overview of specialization methods, we will introduce the most recent developments, such as (among others): handling asymmetric relations (e.g., hypernymy-hyponymy) in Euclidean and hyperbolic spaces by accounting for vector magnitude as well as for vector distance; cross-lingual transfer of semantic specialization for languages without external lexico-semantic resources; downstream effects of specializing distributional vector spaces; injecting external knowledge into unsupervised pretraining architectures such as ELMo or BERT.

Anthology ID:

D19-2007

AUTHOR INDEX

Notes:

Notes:

Notes:

Notes:

Notes:

Notes:

Notes:

Notes:

Association for Computational Linguistics
209 N. Eighth Street
Stroudsburg, Pennsylvania 18360

CURRAN ASSOCIATES INC.
proceedings.com

ISBN 978-1-7138-0069-9